MANAGE YOUR LANGUAGE

COMMUNICATION SKILLS TIPS FOR MANAGEMENT STUDENTS & PROFESSIONALS

DR. T. S. SANTHI

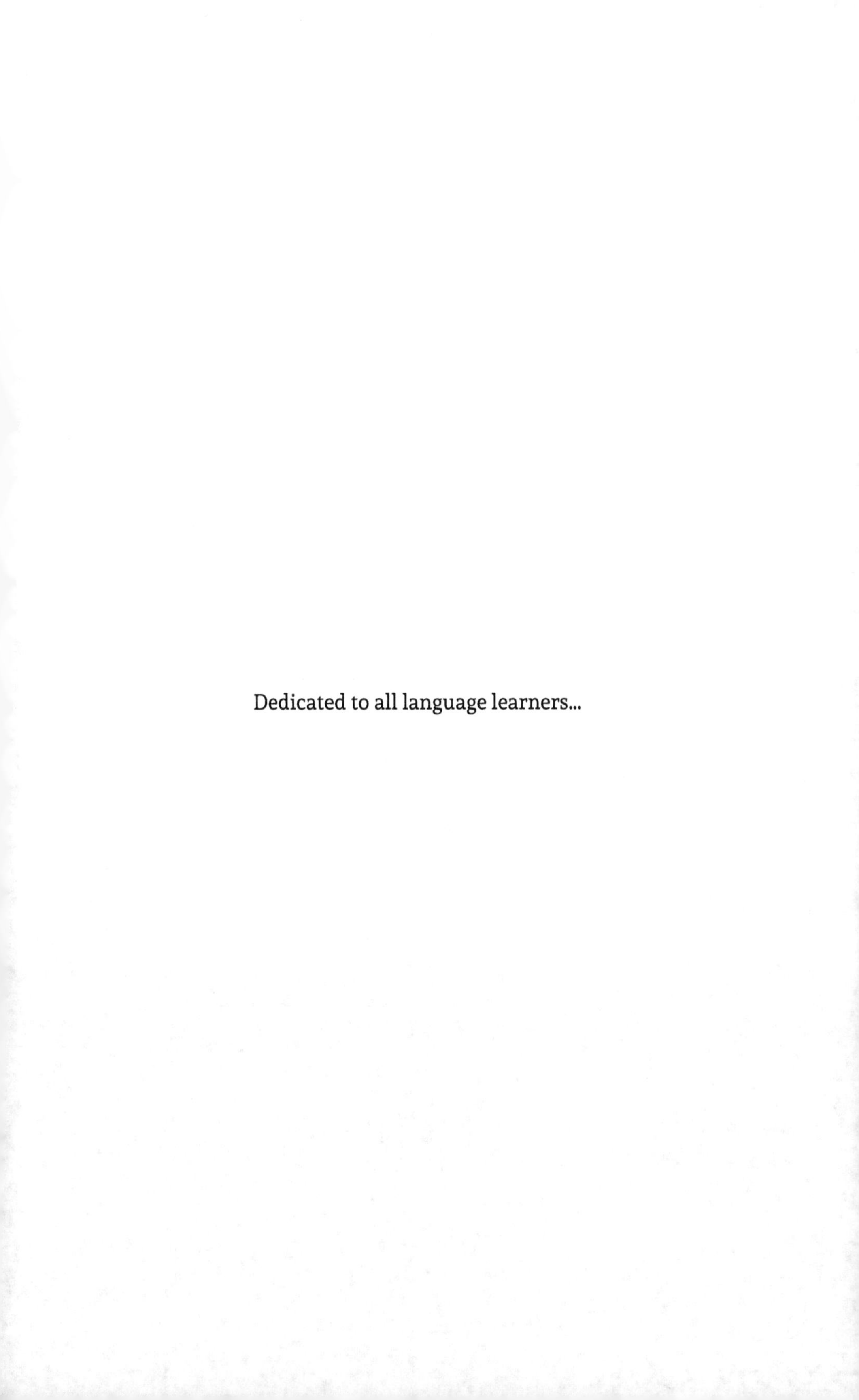

Dedicated to all language learners...

Contents

FOREWORD

It is accepted all over the world that, other than in countries where English is the primary language, India's English is closer to perfection. This is based on people who interact internationally. But it is a sad truth that the majority of the Indian population is quite behind when it comes to speaking English. The problem begins in the very foundation of learning – schools. Schools in India teach English as another subject, just like Math, Science, Social, etc. It is another field to score and boost a child's marks or grades so that the next level of education can be accessed easily. When the foundation is not laid strongly, then one cannot expect the progress of an individual's language to be on par with international standards. Especially when the individual happens to take up managerial positions with poor or mediocre language, not only his reputation but also his company's reputation and performance suffer.

So, what should one do to better one's language? Are there corrective measures?

This book comes as answers to the above questions. It comprises briefs about the four fundamentals of languages – Listening, Speaking, Reading & Writing. Each of these fundamentals is explained, examples from real scenarios are given, and small exercises are given as well.

The intention of bringing out this book is to put language learners at ease, help them with their doubts, and give them ample tips to avoid mistakes and improve their standards. Hope every reader benefits in some way or another. Happy learning!

Preface

Why is this Book Needed?

Every book is drafted and published to take a little bit of learning to the target readers. In the same way, this book too is brought out to promote learning. What sets this one different from other English language teaching books is that while other books are intended for specific readers, this book is for all. This would cater to learners of all levels. A beginner can benefit as much from it, and so can a manager looking for extra material to improve his language.

This book is needed for everyone willing to learn and improve. It does include some theories of grammar and vocabulary, but they are followed immediately by exercises to apply them to check the level of understanding. It also will prove to be a very good extra hand to teachers who coach learners from varied backgrounds and specialisations.

To sum up, the following are the reasons why this book is needed.

- To revise the basics
- Learn the correct usage
- Identify and correct mistakes
- Know varied other usages of the language

The book has four important modules. It covers Listening, Reading, speaking, and Writing – the perfect order to learn a language.

ACKNOWLEDGEMENTS

My sincere thanks to the College Management for their support and encouragement.

Thanks to the team of content editors who worked very hard to bring my thoughts to words.

My love and affection to my friends who stood by me and encouraged me to go with this long-pending idea.

Gratitude to the Almighty for taking me to the right people at the right time to bring this book out.

Prologue

WHAT IS BUSINESS ENGLISH?

Business English refers to the language used for a particular purpose in a specific formal situation. English being the lingua-franca, is shared across the world. To enable a non-native speaker of English to fit well in an international platform to promote his business, this variation of English will be helpful.

Most of the communication that happens in a formal scenario, in offices, business meetings, conferences, and so on, occur among non-native speakers. In such scenarios, the language should be objective. There is absolutely no room for slang or decorative language. The target is to be efficient and effective in communication.

Business English, however, differs from person to person. Some are more concerned about using the perfect vocabulary to fit their trade relations. A few focus on language to improve their skills that can be implemented in their workplaces. Others target distinctive business communication such as presentations, negotiations, meetings, small talk, socializing, e-mail, and report writing.

- To learn beyond basics
- To establish better communication in the workplace
- To deliver effective presentations and reports
- To be travel-ready
- To express oneself better

Whatever the need, with a strong foundation in basics, and a few tips and tricks to use the language effectively, one can ace any situation with ease.

LISTENING

I

LISTEN!

LISTEN!

"I hear you!"

"I'm listening to you!"

What is the difference between the two statements above? Is hearing different from listening?

Of course, yes.

Hearing is the ability to grasp sounds through our ears. The level of sensing sounds depends on the volume produced. It simply is one of the five sensory actions. Our ears can grasp several sounds simultaneously and yet send signals to our brains to distinguish each.

On the other hand, listening is the attention we give to specific sounds. When a person speaks, we don't stop with the sounds made alone. We concentrate on the content conveyed, as well. We try to grasp the ideas conveyed by the person and often come out with a response, either verbal or non-verbal.

While partial hearing or mishearing might not affect a person's response and interactions, partial listening or poor listening will definitely affect a person's reputation with the speaker. Listening is linked with memory. Our brains connect other sounds in the background with the information we listen to. This helps us to recall them when needed.

Thus the action of hearing is different from listening. The next time someone says they can hear you, remember they simply mean you are audible. Their response alone will tell whether or not they listened to the content.

II

LISTENING FOR A SPECIFIC PURPOSE

Listening is a simple process. But it is to be done systematically to be perfect. The sounds made by the speaker have to be understood, the tone of the speaker has to be grasped, and the relevance of the topic spoken must be clear. Only then the desired response is possible.

The famous French theorist Roland Barthes says one can understand the concept of listening at three levels - alerting, deciphering, and understanding.

Alerting refers to detecting the sound. Deciphering means interpreting the sounds. Understanding means the ability to respond correctly to the sounds deciphered.

When a person can understand the speaker and can respond appropriately, the listening is active. It becomes an exchange of ideas between two or more people. The quality of communication will be better. This happens because one listens for a specific purpose. To fulfil the purpose, the individual pays more attention to details and responds accurately.

Sample audio can be found in the link given below.
https://www.ielts.org/about-the-test//-/media/files/listening-sample-task-type-1.ashx

The transcript for the same is below.

You will hear a telephone conversation between a customer and an agent at a company
which ships large boxes overseas.

A: Good morning Packham's Shipping Agents. Can I help you?

B: Oh yes, I'm ringing to make enquiries about sending a large box, a container,
back home to Kenya from the UK.

A: Yes, of course. Would you like me to try and find some quotations for you?

B: Yes, that'd be great. Thank you.

A: Well first of all, I need a few details from you.

B: Fine.

A: Can I take your name?

B: It's Jacob Mkere.

A: Can you spell your surname, please?

B: Yes, it's M-K-E-R-E.

A: Is that 'M' for mother?

B: Yes.

A: Thank you, and you say that you will be sending the box to Kenya?

B: That's right.

A: And where would you like the box picked up from?

B: From college, if possible.

A: Yes, of course. I'll take down the address now.

B: It's Westall College.

A: Is that W-E-S-T-A-L-L?

B: Yes, ... college.

A: Westall College. And where's that?

It's Downlands Road, in Bristol.

A: Oh yes, I know it. And the postcode?

B: It's BS8 9PU.

A: Right ... and I need to know the size.

B: Yes, I've measured it carefully and it's 1.5m long ...

A: Right.

B: 0.75m wide ...

A: OK.

B: And it's 0.5m high or deep.

A: Great. So I'll calculate the volume in a moment and get some quotes for that. But
first can you tell me, you know, very generally, what will be in the box?
B: Yes there's mostly clothes.
A: OK. [writing down]
B: And there's some books.
A: OK. Good. Um ... Anything else?
B: Yes, there's also some toys.
A: OK and what is the total value, do you think, of the contents?
B: Well the main costs are the clothes and the books – they'll be about £1500 but
then the toys are about another two hundred – so I'd put down £1700.
Based on the audio, a sample test is given below. Try filling out the missing information.

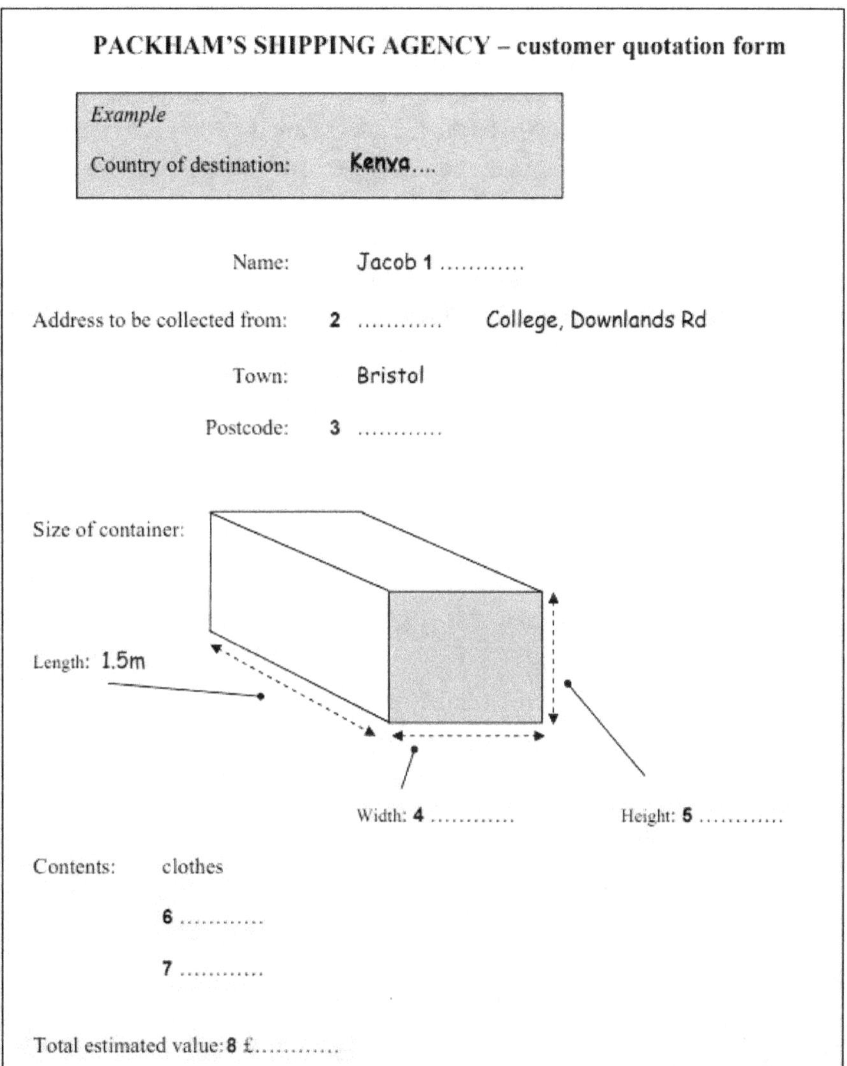

Fill in the blanks based on the audio/transcript.

The first time you listen to the audio, you just listen to grasp the situation and tone. You might not give much attention to finer details. But, when questions are raised based on the audio, your attention is greater the next time you listen to the file. You try to catch every small number, name, and detail.

This sample will give you an idea of how to listen, retain, and remember the details. Thus active listening is triggered. Next time you listen to a speaker, remember that the person expects you to remember the details of his speech.

More audio tests can be found in Sample test questions (ielts.org).
Do listen to the audio files and try your hand with the tests. It will give you the confidence to face an actual IELTS test.

III
WORKPLACE LISTENING

Listening should ideally result in an active response. Without appropriate responses, a speaker cannot proceed further. Responses are keys to suggesting active listening. This is a very important point to be remembered in every day listening. But more so in the workplace.

A workplace where a person is vested with responsibilities when fulfilled properly is often rewarded. A superior is not just a person in command. He is supposed to be the driving force of an entire team. He should be an ideal example to his peers and reporting employees. He is often recognized for his achievements only when he has a special place in the good books of other employees. For this the first step is to listen actively to everyone.

Listening skills are important for career success, organizational effectiveness, and employee satisfaction. Listening in the workplace includes understanding the speaker's intention, accurate interpretation of the ideas conveyed, proper evaluation of the inputs, taking necessary actions as soon as possible, and taking steps to avoid any miscommunication.

The following is a conversation between a manager and his subordinate. Read through and notice how each differs in their tones.

A: "Hi Harry, I finished the assignment on the documents. Did you get a chance to review them?"

B: "Yeah. I already reviewed them. It was pretty good."

A: "Since it was my first project, I was wondering if I can get some feedback."

B: "Well, you finished the project on time. And seeing how it was your first assignment, you did very well."

A: "Thanks. If it wasn't my first assignment, where do you think I need to improve?"

B: "That's a fair question... I think you could have spent a little more time documenting the difference between Process A and Process B. You showed a lot of the similarities, but lacking a little on the differences."

A: "I'll keep that in mind. How about the structure? I changed the template a little because I wanted to add a section for recommendation."

B: "I liked the addition. Usually people just enter it into the comment section on the bottom but having a clear section makes it stand out. That was good."

A: "Was there anything else? I like to get feedback early so I can improve."

B: "No problem. Everything else on the assignment was great. The only other tip I can give you is sending me more updates. If I knew you were stuck on section C for a while, I could have saved you a lot of time. So keep me aware on your status."

A: "That makes sense. I'll do that. Thanks for the feedback."

B: "Don't mention it. And good job on the assignment."

A: "Thanks."

The above conversation shows how well A and B listened to one another. Their responses are accurate to the information asked and the feedback given. This is a good example of active listening in workplace.

Active listening makes you popular because you are paying attention to the person and trying to understand, build trust and empathize before giving solutions and recommendations. This makes a person a good team player.

IV
EFFECTIVE LISTENING

How do I test if a person listened or not? How do I test myself if I listened to another speaker properly?

Here are a few points to our aid.

1) ASK QUESTIONS

You may raise doubts or ask for suggestions to check if the other person is listening to you.

Example: *What is your opinion on project A? You mentioned point B; can you elaborate on it?*

2) ACKNOWLEDGE & APPRECIATE

Quote words or phrases from the speaker's contents. Nod, smile, and reply positively to small questions. Slide in appreciative phrases like *"that was an excellent point"*, *"well said"*, or *"I totally agree with you"*. This straightaway suggest you were listening actively.

3) MAKE EYE CONTACT WITH THE SPEAKER

The best nonverbal gesture to assure your active listening is through proper eye contact. DO NOT STARE! Just gaze into the speaker's eyes and let your acknowledgement flow without words.

HOW TO IMPROVE MY LISTENING SKILLS?

Listening is actually difficult since the human attention span is very less. In that case, how do I make sure I am ready to face questions or contribute to a content proactively? Here are a few tips to improve your listening skills.

1) **Take notes** - take down important facts, data, and key information that might be points of discussion later.

2) **Remember clues** - important information is often accompanied by examples or illustrations. Remember the examples, you will remember the points.

3) **Ask questions** - If the speaker permits, ask questions and get your doubts clarified immediately. If not, note down the question and ensure it is addressed after the speaker is done.

THE BEST WAY TO PRACTISE LISTENING

One of the easiest ways to improve one's listening skills is by watching English shows and movies WITHOUT subtitles. LISTEN to the dialogues spoken by the native speakers. Register their responses and try to train your ears to the sounds of native English.

Happy listening!

V
LISTENING EXERCISES

The following websites can be referred to attempt listening exercises on various topics. The audio will be followed by questions.

All the best!

1. English Listening Exercises - Online Lessons for ESL Students (esolcourses.com)

2. 5 ESL Listening Exercises to Sharpen Your Students' Ears | FluentU English Educator Blog

3. Listening | esl-lounge Student

4. Listening | LearnEnglish (britishcouncil.org)

5. English Listening - Listening lessons ESL students with audio files and fun questions (talkenglish.com)

SPEAKING

Enter Caption

VI
SPEAK!

Human beings' most effective tool of communication is SPEECH. While it is easy to interact with friends and family, it is always difficult to talk or even begin a conversation with strangers. The following are some of the reasons why people hesitate to talk.

- Lack of confidence
- Fear of judgement
- Unsure about language potential

- Afraid of unknown subjects

How to overcome the above setbacks?

- Trust your instincts
- Do not bother about other people's judgement
- As long your language is understood by your friends and family, it will surely be understood by others too
- Be objective and not subjective while talking

Official interactions start the moment you talk to an organisation's representative to fix the interview date. Few common DOs and DON'Ts will help us in a long run.

DOs

1. Be confident (Frank about your talents. But not boastful)
2. Be polite (Use expressions like Sorry, Please, May I..., Would you mind...)
3. Keep your statements short
4. Answer TO the question, not to the person
5. Be honest about topics that you are not aware of

DON'Ts

1. Do not beat around the bush
2. Do not sound overtly sweet or overtly blunt
3. Do not answer with a single word (Like Yes, Yeah, No.... Make sure an explanation follows)
4. Do not lie about details (Especially technical skills and attitude which can always be checked at a later stage)
5. Do not make lengthy statements

More tips and tricks are to follow in the upcoming chapters. But, most of all, SPEAK! Grab opportunities and speak sensibly. The more you speak, the better your language becomes.

Happy speaking!

VII
ART OF SPEAKING

Why is speaking an art?

Speaking is an art because it must be crafted and delivered carefully and creatively. Great communication must be prepared, formatted and expressed with excellence and eloquence.

Speaking does not mean one will have to hold a microphone and address a huge gathering. It can be a formal deliverance or a semi-formal presentation to a small group of colleagues. In organisations, managers often require presenting data or reports to their colleagues or subordinates. These presentations might happen weekly or monthly on a small scale, and sometimes a quarterly presentation to higher officials or important clients.

So, how does one speak? How to master the art of speaking to any gathering?

STEP 1: INNOVATE

Every fact known to mankind is presented in some form or other. Why are a few successful while others fail? It is simply because the successful ones are innovative. They cater to the interest of the audience.

"You need not do different things; just do things differently." goes a popular saying.

Use catchy idioms, phrases, visual aids, illustrations, and attractive methods to support your speech or presentation.

STEP 2: ARRANGE

Arrange your ideas in such a way that the audience can understand where the speech is heading. Go one step at a time. Let there be a connection between one point to the next one. This will not only keep the audience engaged but also on track.

STEP 3: STYLIZE

Be causal in deliverance. Be yourself. Trying to imitate, using a false accent of English, and using unknown vocabulary will only pull the performance down. The original you stay, the more your effort will be appreciated. So, when we say "Stylize", we simply ask you to retain your style.

STEP 4: TOOLS TO THE AID

Use tools like projectors or smart screens to project your visual aids. Prepare PowerPoint presentations, charts, graphs, short videos, or animations to make your content appealing and interesting. It is also a great way to retain audience's attention.

Below are a few collections of collages of popular business idioms taken from esl.com. Go on, try them the next time you step up for a presentation.

Business Idioms: Leadership

(The) Man

The boss; authority in general

Ahead Of The Curve

Offering ideas not yet in general circulation; highly creative

Big Picture

A wide perspective; a broad view of something

Changing of the Guard

A change in leadership at an organization

Call the Shots

Make the important decisions in an organization

Cut Someone Some Slack

Avoid treating someone strictly or severely

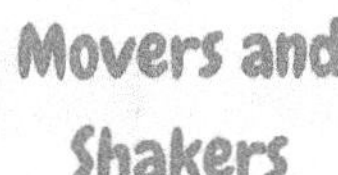

Movers and Shakers

Influential people, especially in a particular field

Rake Someone Over the Coals

Scold severely

Light a Fire Under Someone

Inspire someone to work very hard

1

Business Idioms: Decision

On the Same Page

Understanding a situation in the same way

All Things Considered

Taking all factors into consideration

Fish or Cut Bait

Make a decision or give someone else a chance.

Up for Grabs

Available

Up in the Air

Not yet decided

Raise Red Flags

Warn of trouble ahead

Out of the Loop

Not part of a group that's kept informed about something

All Things Being Equal

In the event that all aspects of a situation remain the same.

Flip-Flop

To vacillate between two choices, to be indecisive

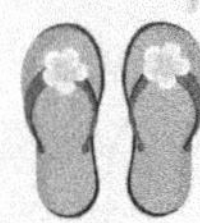

ESL COM

2

Business Idioms: Money

Nickel and dime
To negotiate over very small sums

A penny saved is a penny earned

Every small amount helps to build one's savings

Banner Year
A year marked by strong successes

Dime a dozen
Very common and of no special value; easily available

Crunch the Numbers
Do calculations before making a decision or prediction.

In the Red
Losing money, below a specified starting point
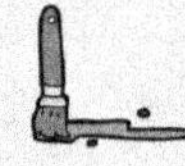

Nest Egg
Retirement savings; wealth saved for a future purpose

You Can Take It to the Bank
I absolutely guarantee this.

Pinch pennies
To be careful with money, to be thrify

ESL COM

3

Business Idioms: Jobs

Get the Sack

To be fired

Hanging by a Thread

In great danger of elimination or failure

Off the Hook

Free from blame or responsibility to do something

Rank and File

The ordinary members of an organization

Move Up in the World

Become more successful

Out of Work

Unemployed

Give Someone The Old Heave-Ho

Fire someone, remove someone from a group or team

Pink Slip

A layoff notice; loss of a job, typically because of layoffs

Burn the Candle at Both Ends

Work very long hours

ESL COM

4

Business Idioms: Negotiation

Trial Balloon
A test of someone's or the public's reaction

Back And Forth
Dialogue, negotiations

An Offer One Can't Refuse
An extremely attractive offer

Come to Terms With
Feel acceptance toward something bad that has happened

Draw a Line in the Sand
Issue an ultimatum; specify an absolute limit in a conflict

Drive a Hard Bargain
To negotiate effectively

Give and Take
Negotiations, the process of compromise

Sweeten the Deal
Add something to an offer during a negotiation

Stand One's Ground
Refuse to back down; insist on one's position

5

Business Idioms: Problems

In Hot Water
In need of help; in trouble

Head (Go) South
Decline, get worse

(An) Uphill Climb
A difficult process

Red Tape
Difficult bureaucratic or governmental requirements

(The) Last Straw
A problem or insult that finally demands a response

Above Water
Not in extreme difficulty. Especially said of finances.

Cut Corners
Economize by reducing quality; take shortcuts

Think Outside the Box
Try to solve a problem in an original way; think creatively

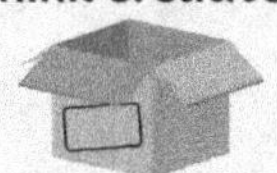

In a Jam
In need of help, in a difficult spot

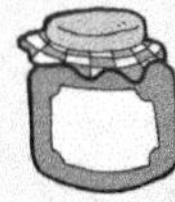

ESL COM

6

Business Idioms: Sales and Marketing

In the Pipeline
Being prepared for the marketplace, being worked on.

Sold On (Something)
Convinced of something

Deliver the Goods
Provide what is expected

Out the Door
With everything included (said of a price)

Price yourself out of the market
Try to sell goods or services at such a high price that nobody buys them.

Sell (Someone) a Bill of Goods
Trick someone; be deceptive

Selling Point
An attractive feature of something for sale

All It's Cracked Up To Be
As good as claims or reputation would suggest

TLC
Tender Loving Care

ESL COM

7

Business Idioms: Schedule

By the Book
According to established procedure

Pencil Something In
Make tentative arrangements

Against The Clock
Forced to hurry to meet a deadline

Back to the Drawing Board
Forced to begin something again

Busman's Holiday
A working vacation

Burn the Midnight Oil
Working late into the night

Back to the Salt Mines
It's time for me (us) to go back to work.

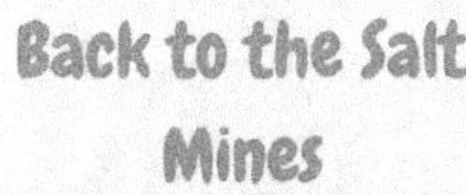

Eleventh Hour
The last minute

In the Works
Under development; coming soon

ESL COM

8

• 29 •

VIII
TIPS TO IMPROVE SPEAKING

There is no ZERO level in speaking. Whatever we learnt in school will make us stand at least in level two if not higher. All we need to do is build on the basics we learnt. Here are some common mistakes and their corrections. Avoid these, and you will already be up a level higher.

1) *I can able to understand. (NO)*
I can understand. (YES)
2) *I could not able to finish. (NO)*
I could not finish. (YES)

Explanation: "Could/Can" are called MODAL VERBS. They are used to convey a specific purpose - ABILITY. Adding an "able" after either of these words will make the sentence look like this.

I can can understand. I am able able to understand.
AVOID the above usage.

3) *We was doing well last year. (NO)*
We were doing well last year. (YES)
4) *You was very helpful. (NO)*
You were very helpful. (YES)

Explanation: Like in other languages, English has a set of rules for using pronouns with verbs. The following table will come handy the next time you decide to use one of them.

5) *We are one of the top company in the industry. (NO)*
We are one of the top companies in the industry. (YES)

Explanation: The phrase "one of the" should be followed by a PLURAL noun ONLY. You can be singled only when in a group!

Subject Verb Agreement				
Pronoun	Positive	Positive Contraction	Negative	Negative Contraction
I	I am	I'm	I am not	I'm not
you	you are	You're	you are not	You're not
he	he is	he's	he is not	he's not
she	she is	she's	she is not	she's not
it	it is	it's	it is not	it's not
we	we are	we're	we are not	we're not
they	they are	they're	they are not	they're not

Pronouns - Verbs agreement (CONCORD)

6) *Can I tell the answer? (NO)*

May I tell you the answer? (YES)

Explanation: "Can" denotes ability. "May" denotes seeking permission. While the intention may be understood, it still is inappropriate in official scenarios. "May" is polite and safe to use. The below table will clarify the usage of MODALS while speaking.

English Modal Verbs – Situations Table

Situation	Modal Verb	Example
Requests (formal)	May	May I sit down?
Requests (informal)	Can	Can I sit down?
Requests (polite)	Could	Could I sit down?
Requests (polite)	Would	Would you mind if I sit down?
Permission (formal)	May	You may sit down.
Permission (informal)	Can	You can sit down.
Obligation (full)	Must	You must tell the police the truth.
Obligation (partial)	Should	You should tell your friends the truth.
Obligation (partial) (less common)	Ought to	You ought to tell your friends the truth.
Logical conclusions (stronger than "should")	Must	He left an hour ago, so he must be there already.
Logical conclusions (weaker than "must")	Should	He left half an hour ago, I believe he should be there already.
Possibility (general)	Can	It can rain sometimes.
Possibility (weaker than "may" and "might")	Could	It could rain, but it is not very common in this part of the country.
Possibility (weaker than "may")	Might	It's not very cloudy yet, but it might rain.
Possibility (stronger than "might")	May	It starts getting cloudy – it may rain soon.
Future actions/states/intentions	Will	Look at the sky! It will rain soon.

Another important point to remember while speaking is always to KISS your content. Now, do not get confused. It simply means to Keep It Short and Straight. The shorter the sentences you use, the straighter the ideas are conveyed, and the better the audience retention and understanding.

Issues that surround pronunciation:

The desire to learn English is not something very new. It has been one of the top priorities of every Indian. Parents are always proud when their children address them 'mummy' and 'daddy' which is not the case if the same is done in their mother tongue. They prefer to put their wards in English medium schools hoping the children would be taught the popular language of the age. Learning a language is nothing but imitation of sounds. Children imitate what is taught to them in schools. The English teacher plays a vital role in introducing and teaching the new language. In order to train the child's ears to accept the new language, they begin with teaching simple, yet interesting method – rhymes recitation. What the child grasps at an early age is developed over years, with constant drilling and usage. At later stages, at the time of stepping into their career, children realize the importance of knowing English. Children, who miss out on learning the language to the fullest possible extent at the early stages, find themselves in a fix later. Every company today demands candidates who are fluent in speaking English. Though they do not expect candidates to speak like an Englishman, but they expect them to have a neutralized accent. Thus comes in the importance of pronouncing words properly, if not accurately, for words mispronounced will always lead to misconception, misinterpretation and even ridicule.

A message intended to be communicated, must be put with appropriate words. Appropriate usage alone will not make the communication effective. The words used must be pronounced appropriately too.

For example: The teacher **beat** the student.

If the word 'beat' is not properly pronounced; if the /i:/ sound is not elongated, then it will be conveyed as 'The teacher **bit** the student', which not only is ridiculous, but also absurd and conveys a very violent meaning.

Though a person at work might be efficient in typing out letters and memos, if he fails to address a group efficiently, he is looked down as an inefficient person. Speaking with appropriate pronunciation is a must for teachers, help-desk executives, call-centre executives, public speakers, telephone operators, public announcers and everyone in general. In the case of professionals who need to constantly interact with native English speakers, it becomes more than necessary to pronounce words to perfection, for what sounds perfect to us might sound odd or misappropriate to a native speaker of English.

For example, the following conversation between a call-centre executive and an American client illustrates the same –

Client: *Don't you guys make any of those special model equipment anymore?*

Executive: *No sir. The demand for the equipment has down of late. So we make no more of it.*

In the above conversation, the client mistook the phrase 'of late' as 'half plate'. He was not able to comprehend why the executive mentioned half plate.

India has a wide variety of languages which in turn take up plenty of dialects. Since English is only taught as a second language, the learners tend to connote the language to their mother tongue. The mind, as and when English is spoken, does a quick translation and makes sense to the listener who is a non-native speaker of English. Hence, whatever amount of English is understood and spoken by a non-native speaker is nothing but the result of the mental translation that went on earlier. Therefore, every non-native speaker tends to lean over his mother tongue for support. Though the leaning-over-mother-tongue factor helps a learner get into the language quickly and effectively, it hinders his spontaneous learning to a certain extent. It prevents the learner from thinking in English. It provokes him to translate whenever possible. Sometimes this practice makes the learner to use wrong sentence patterns or misuse words and expressions, thereby degrading his English to a considerable amount. The mother tongue not only hinders learning of words and sentence patterns, but also pronunciation. Not all the languages have got the same set of speech sounds. What is present in one language might not be available in other languages.

For example: the sound / ʃ / is not available in Indian languages. Hence it is always substituted with **/z/** or **/s/**

Education,/edjʊkeiʃən/ is often pronounced as **/edjʊkeizən/** in North India and **/edjʊkeisən/** in South India.

The vowel sound **/æ/** as in '**apple**' is often pronounced as **/ei/** as in '**ape**' in North India and as **/a:/** as in '**arm**' in South India.

Pronunciation is one of the most difficult areas for Indian Students. All Indian students find it difficult to produce certain individual sounds, both vowel and consonant.

For example: the pronunciation of 'z' is also difficult for an Indian. A North Indian pronounces 'zoo' as 'joo', whereas a South Indian pronounces it as 'soo'.

They also find it difficult to differentiate between 'v' and 'w'. All these problems arise because there are no such sounds in any of the Indian languages.

For example: the words like 'which', 'wear', 'where', 'what' are pronounced as 'vich', 'vere'.

A minority of Indian students also find it difficult to differentiate between voiced and voiceless consonants.

Another major challenge in pronunciation is word stress. Indians invariably stress the wrong syllable in a word, which makes it difficult for a native English speaker to understand them, and vice versa.

For example: the words like 'photographer', 'photography', 'psychology' are stressed on the second syllable. But Indians tend to stress the first or third syllable of these words.

Any of the native varieties of English is a stress-timed language, and word stress is an important feature of Received Pronunciation. Indian native languages are actually syllable-timed languages. Indian English speakers usually speak with a syllabic rhythm. Further, in some Indian languages, stress is associated with a low pitch, whereas in most English dialects, stressed syllables are generally pronounced with a higher pitch. Thus, when Indian speakers speak, they appear to put the stress accents at the wrong syllables, or accentuate all the syllables of a long English word. The Indian accent is a 'sing-song' accent.

The TESOL teacher should have a good knowledge of how the suprasegmentals are employed in English. Suprasegmentals are those sounds which are overlaid on segmentals. These do not occur without segmental which carry them.

Stress, rhythm, and intonation are the three important elements of the suprasegmental system used in English.

Some syllables may be pronounced with more force or intensity than others. This is called stress. English is a free stress language, unlike French in which the stress always falls on the last syllable of utterance. In English the stress can be placed on any syllable of the utterance in order to achieve a variety of purpose. The meaning of single words can be changed by shifting the stress. Words which are not ordinarily stressed may be stressed for emphasis.

Problems surrounding pronunciation are common among non-native speakers. But the problems are not too complex. Constant drilling and practice can surely bring in notable improvement in the learners' language.

Initially the use of words and their pronunciation must be made consciously. Later on it will become a part of speaking trend. If errors from a part of our language, even if we consciously try to rectify them, we will not be able to do it efficiently.

Exercises, tests, speech therapy, etc. are few techniques that will ensure good pronunciation. In order to master a language, the learner must not only speak, read and write it, but also must think using the language. Mental translation is something done unconsciously. But conscious avoidance of the same will ensure we think only in English, thus helping us master the language.

IX
PRACTISE

SCENE 1: Introduction

Q - Let's talk about your home town or village.

A - Include the following points in your answer.

• What kind of place is it?

• What's the most interesting part of your town/village?

• What kind of jobs do the people in your town/village do?

• Would you say it's a good place to live? (Why?)

EXAMPLE:

Examiner: Now, in this first part, I'd like to ask you some more questions about yourself, OK? Let's talk about your home town or village. What kind of place is it?

Candidate: It's quite a small village, about 20km from Chennai. And it's very quiet. And we have only little … two little shops because most of the people work in the city or are orientated to the city.

Examiner: What's the most interesting part of this place … village?

Candidate: There is a small hill. On the top of a hill we have a castle which is very old and quite well known.

Examiner: What kind of jobs do people in the village do?

Candidate: We mostly have farmers in the village. We also have bankers, teachers and some doctors.

Examiner: Would you say it's a good place to live?

Candidate: Yes. Although it is very quiet, it is … people are friendly, and I would say it is a good place to live there, yes.

SCENE 2: Descriptions

Q - Describe a tourist spot you enjoyed visiting.

A - Include the following points in your answer.

· Exact location of the place and how to reach the place

· What's the most interesting part of the spot?

· What are the major places of attraction there?

· Why do you recommend the place?

EXAMPLE:

I like to travel whenever I get the chance and have the means to afford the costs. I would like to share my experience of travelling to a lovely beach, which is one of the most popular tourist destinations in our city.

The name of this tourist spot is "Sky blue beach" - a natural beach with mesmerising views located along the East Coast Road. It offers a diverse range of activities for tourists of all ages. You can just idly lay on the beach and enjoy the clear blue sky, crystal clear sea water, synchronised tide and ebb, and listen to the music of the gentle breeze all day long without worrying about other things!

I visited this attractive spot almost a year ago, just after my semester break. I did not want to miss the chance to spend some quality time away from the hustle and bustle of city life. I thought it would be refreshing and invigorating, and I was proven right. Just after I reached there, I thought I was taken to a dreamworld!

I enjoyed the view the most. It was like nothing else that I had ever experienced. The calm nature of the surroundings, floating breeze of the coast, vast ocean, soft sandy beach, blue sky and the vast openness blew away my mind. I also enjoyed some local foods, tried a boat ride, enjoyed some music concerts at night, and did some barbecue parties with my friends.

I believe I relished visiting this tourist attraction because it was a marvellous beach area with lots of things to see and do. I enjoyed a relaxing, soothing and peaceful vacation after a long and the experience was so charming that I liked it a lot. This was the first time when I realised how nature holds so many different kinds of beauty that could equally thrill and excite us.

SCENE 3: Interview

The following are a few commonly asked questions in interviews. They are followed by points that are to be remembered while answering an interviewer.

Q - *Tell me about yourself.*

DON'T talk about your personal details that are already there on your resume.

DO talk about your skills and what makes you an efficient person.

Q - *What is your biggest weakness?*

DON'T deny your weakness. DON'T brag about your weakness.

DO be subtle about your weakness and ADD how you are working to overcome the same.

Q - *Why should I hire you?*

DON'T project yourself as an irreplaceable candidate.

DO stress on your skills that set your apart.

Q - *Do you have any questions for me?*

DON'T avoid asking questions. DON'T ask irrelevant questions.

DO enquire about the finer details of the job description like work timings, other skills needed to meet the expectations, etc.

READING

Enter Caption

X
READ!

Reading opens an all-new world. People might come out with suggestions like "read newspapers", "read motivational books", "read this book by so-and-so", and many more. Here is a tip.

READ WHAT INTERESTS YOU THE MOST.

A book is a good source of language learning, no matter what genre it belongs to. As long as it does not carry too much slang, any book is just fine. Today every book is available in e-format too. So, if you feel lazy to open a book, just open an ebook.

Reading is of two main types. Intensive reading and extensive reading.

Intensive reading is when you get engrossed in a book, read every word in it, try to understand every concept, and recollect the information after you finish reading. It might not necessarily be for an exam. It might simply be because of the interest the book created in you.

Extensive reading is when you are interested in one particular topic, find more books on the same, and read them all. Again, it might be a serious topic or just fiction belonging to one particular theme.

Without much giving thought about the theoretical part of reading, just grab a book and start reading. If one book does not interest you, try another. Keep trying until you find the right one. But, do not every stop reading.

READING FOR ORGANISATIONAL PURPOSE

Official reading demands more attention. The focus has to be more on the facts and data presented. Organisational reading would include reading official emails, memos, circulars, reports, etc.

How does reading help an individual in an organisation?

- broadens the perspective of the individual,
- improves the speed of grasping contents,
- enables understanding of new words and structures
- develops an eye for cues
- helps in retaining contents for a longer period

[Note: The following passage is an extract from a Part 3 text about the 'Plain English' movement, which promotes the use of clear English.] 'The Cambridge Encyclopedia of Language', David Crystal, 3rd Edition, © Cambridge University Press, 2010.

The instructions accompanying do-it-yourself products are regularly cited as a source of unnecessary expense or frustration. Few companies seem to test their instructions by having them followed by a first-time user. Often, essential information is omitted, steps in the construction process are taken for granted, and some special knowledge is assumed. This is especially worrying in fields where failure to follow correct procedures can be dangerous. Objections to material in plain English have come mainly from the legal profession. Lawyers point to the risk of ambiguity inherent in everyday language for legal or official documents and draw attention to the need for confidence in legal formulations, which can come only from using language tested in courts over centuries. The campaigners point out that there has been no sudden increase in litigation due to the increase in basic English materials.

Similarly, professionals in several fields have defended their use of technical and complex language as the most precise means of expressing technical or complex ideas. This is undoubtedly true: scientists, doctors, bankers and others need their jargon to communicate succinctly and unambiguously. But when it comes to addressing the non-specialist consumer, the campaigners argue, different criteria must apply.

Based on the passage, try completing the summary given below.

Consumers often complain that they experience a feeling of 1 .... when trying to put together do-it-yourself products which have not been tested by companies on a 2 .... In situations where not keeping to the correct procedures could affect safety issues, it is especially important that 3 .... information is not left out and no assumptions are made about a stage being self-evident or the consumer having a certain amount of 4 .... Lawyers, however, have raised objections to the use of plain English. They feel that it would result in ambiguity in documents and cause people to lose faith in 5 .... , as it would mean departing from language that has been used in the courts for a very long time.

The summary will give an idea of what to look for while reading a content. Thus, the following are a few practices to be followed consciously while reading.

- mental summarising
- guessing and analysing
- understanding contextual meanings of words
- filtering out cliches and retaining important information

Happy reading!

XI
READING COMPREHENSION

Reading comprehension enhances the reading skills and improves the level of comprehension in ones mind. The strategy for reading comprehension is the technique called SQ3R. This stands for Survey, Question, Read, Recite, and Review. This type of exercise will help one infer meanings by simply reading the text and understanding the situations involved.

Given below are few passages for reading comprehension. Read the passages and answer the questions given below each of them.

Exercise 1:

THE GREAT WALL OF CHINA

Walls and wall building have played a very important role in Chinese culture. These people, from the dim mists of prehistory have been wall-conscious; from the Neolithic period – when ramparts of pounded earth were used - to the Communist Revolution, walls were an essential part of any village. Not only towns and villages; the houses and the temples within them were somehow walled, and the houses also had no windows overlooking the street, thus giving the feeling of wandering around a huge maze. The name for "city" in Chinese (ch'eng) means wall, and over these walled cities, villages, houses and temples presides the god of walls and mounts, whose duties were, and still are, to protect and be responsible for the welfare of the inhabitants. Thus a great and extremely laborious task such as constructing a wall, which was supposed to run throughout the country, must not have seemed such an absurdity.

However, it is indeed a common mistake to perceive the Great Wall as a single architectural structure, and it would also be erroneous to assume that it was built during a single dynasty. For the building of the wall spanned the various dynasties, and each of these dynasties somehow contributed to the refurbishing and the construction of a wall, whose foundations had been laid many centuries ago. It was during the fourth and third century B.C. that each warring state started building walls to protect their kingdoms, both against one another and against the northern nomads. Especially three of these states: the Ch'in, the Chao and the Yen, corresponding respectively to the modern provinces of Shensi, Shanzi and Hopei, over and above building walls that surrounded their kingdoms, also laid the foundations on which Ch'in Shih Huang Di would build his first continuous Great Wall.

The role that the Great Wall played in the growth of Chinese economy was an important one. Throughout the centuries many settlements were established along the new border. The garrison troops were instructed to reclaim wasteland and to plant crops on it, roads and canals were built, to mention just a few of the works carried out. All these undertakings greatly helped to increase the country's trade and cultural exchanges with many remote areas and also with the southern, central and western parts of Asia – the formation of the Silk Route. Builders, garrisons, artisans, farmers and peasants left behind a trail of objects, including inscribed tablets, household articles, and written work, which have become extremely valuable archaeological evidence to the study of defence institutions of the Great Wall and the everyday life of these people who lived and died along the wall.

Choose the best answer:

1. Chinese cities resembled a maze

   a. because they were walled.
   b. because the houses has no external windows.
   c. because the name for cities means 'wall'.
   d. because walls have always been important there.

1. Constructing a wall that ran the length of the country

   a. honoured the god of walls and mounts.
   b. was an absurdly laborious task.
   c. may have made sense within Chinese culture.
   d. made the country look like a huge maze.

3. The Great Wall of China

   a. was built in a single dynasty.
   b. was refurbished in the fourth and third centuries BC.
   c. used existing foundations.
   d. was built by the Ch'in, the Chao and the Yen.

4. Crops were planted

   a. on wasteland.
   b. to reclaim wasteland.
   c. on reclaimed wasteland.
   d. along the canals.

5. The Great Wall

   a. helped build trade only inside China.
   b. helped build trade in China and abroad.
   c. helped build trade only abroad.
   d. helped build trade only to remote areas.

Write the meanings of the following words:

1. Ramparts 2. Laborious 3. Absurdity 4. Refurbishing 5. Trail

Say TRUE or FALSE:

1. The Great Wall was built by a single dynasty.
2. The foundations were laid the Ch'in, the Chao and the Yen dynasties.
3. The role that the Great Wall played in the growth of Chinese economy was an important one.
4. Builders left a trail of objects that are valuable archaeological evidences.
5. The Great Wall helped China improve its trade.

Exercise 2:

ENGLISH AS A NATIONAL FOREIGN LANGUAGE

India has two national languages for central administrative purposes: Hindi and English. Hindi is the national, official, and main link language of India. English is an associate official language. The Indian Constitution also officially approves twenty-two regional languages for official purposes.

Dozens of distinctly different regional languages are spoken in India, which share many characteristics such as grammatical structure and vocabulary. Apart from these languages, Hindi is used for communication in India. The homeland of Hindi is mainly in the north of India, but it is spoken and widely understood in all urban centers of India. In the southern states of India, where people speak many different languages that are not much related to Hindi, there is more resistance to Hindi, which has allowed English to remain a lingua franca to a greater degree.

Since the early 1600s, the English language has had a toehold on the Indian subcontinent, when the East India Company established settlements in Chennai, Kolkata, and Mumbai, formerly Madras, Calcutta, and Bombay respectively. The historical background of India is never far away from everyday usage of English. India has had a longer exposure to English than any other country which uses it as a second language, its distinctive words, idioms, grammar and rhetoric spreading gradually to affect all places, habits and culture.

In India, English serves two purposes. First, it provides a linguistic tool for the administrative cohesiveness of the country, causing people who speak different languages to become united. Secondly, it serves as a language of wider communication, including a large variety of different people covering a vast area. It overlaps with local languages in certain spheres of influence and in public domains.

Generally, English is used among Indians as a 'link' language and it is the first language for many well-educated Indians. It is also the second language for many who speak more than one language in India. The English language is a tie that helps bind the many segments of our society together. Also, it is a linguistic bridge between the major countries of the world and India.

English has special national status in India. It has a special place in the parliament, judiciary, broadcasting, journalism, and in the education system. One can see a Hindi-speaking teacher giving their students instructions during an educational tour about where to meet and when their bus would leave, but all in English. It means that the language permeates daily life. It is unavoidable and is always expected, especially in the cities.

The importance of the ability to speak or write English has recently increased significantly because English has become the de facto standard. Learning English language has become popular for business, commerce and cultural reasons and especially for internet communications throughout the world. English is a language that has become a standard not because it has been approved by any 'standards' organization but because it is widely used by many information and technology industries and recognized as being standard. The call centre phenomenon has stimulated a huge expansion of internet-related activity, establishing the future of India as a cyber-technological super-power. Modern communications, videos, journals and newspapers on the internet use English and have made 'knowing English' indispensable.

The prevailing view seems to be that unless students learn English, they can only work in limited jobs. Those who do not have basic knowledge of English cannot obtain good quality jobs. They cannot communicate efficiently with others, and cannot have the benefit of India's rich social and cultural life. Men and women who cannot comprehend and interpret instructions in English, even if educated, are unemployable. They cannot help with their children's school homework everyday or decide their revenue options of the future.

A positive attitude to English as a national language is essential to the integration of people into Indian society. There would appear to be virtually no disagreement in the community about the importance of English language skills. Using English you will become a citizen of the world almost naturally. English plays a dominant role in the media. It has been used as a medium for inter-state communication and broadcasting both before and since India's independence. India is, without a doubt, committed to English as a national language. The impact of English is not only continuing but increasing.

Choose the best answer:

1. According to the writer, the Indian constitution recognises

a. 22 official languages.
b. Hindi as the national language.
c. 2 national, official languages.
d. 2 national languages.

2. English's status as a lingua franca is helped by

a. its status in northern India.
b. the fact that it is widely understood in urban centres.
c. the fact that people from the south speak languages not much related to Hindi.
d. it shares many grammatical similarities with Hindi.

3. In paragraph 3, 'toehold' means that English

a. dominated India.
b. changed the names of some cities in India.
c. has had a presence in India.
d. has been in India longer than any other language.

4. Hindi-speaking teachers

a. might well be heard using English.
b. only use English.
c. only use English for instructions.
d. do not use English.

5. English in India

a. is going to decrease.
b. has decreased since independence.

c. causes disagreement.

d. is going to have a greater importance.

Say TRUE or FALSE:

1. The Indian Constitution approved 25 regional languages for official purposes.
2. English does not hold a special status in India.
3. The importance of the ability to speak or write English has recently decreased significantly because English has become the de facto standard.
4. Those who do not have basic knowledge of English cannot obtain good quality jobs.
5. English plays a dominant role in the media.

Write the meanings of the words:

1. Resistance 2) exposure 3) cohesive 4) phenomenon 5) dominant

Exercise 3:
BIOFUELS AND THE ENVIRONMENT

Leading investors have joined the growing chorus of concern about governments and companies rushing into producing biofuels as a solution for global warming, saying that many involved in the sector could be jeopardising future profits if they do not consider the long-term impact of what they are doing carefully.

It is essential to build sustainability criteria into the supply chain of any green fuel project in order to ensure that there is no adverse effect on the surrounding environment and social structures. The report produced by the investors expresses concern that many companies may not be fully aware of the potential pitfalls in the biofuel sector.

Production of corn and soya beans has increased dramatically in the last years as an eco-friendly alternative to fossil fuels but environmental and human rights campaigners are worried that this will lead to destruction of rain forests. Food prices could also go up as there is increasedcompetition for crops as both foodstuffs and sources of fuel. Last week, the UN warned that biofuels could have dangerous side effects and said that steps need to be taken to make sure that land converted to grow biofuels does not damage the environment or cause civil unrest. There is already great concern about palm oil, which is used in many foods in addition to being an important biofuel, as rain forests are being cleared in some countries and people driven from their homes to create palm oil plantations.

An analyst and author of the investors' report says that biofuels are not a cure for climate change but they can play their part as long as governments and companies manage the social and environmental impacts thoroughly. There should also be greater measure taken to increase efficiency and to reduce demand.

Choose the best answer:

1. _____ are worried about the boom in biofuels.

a. Few people
b. Many people
c. Only these leading investors

2. Biofuel producers _____ know about the possible problems.

a. do not
b. might not
c. must not

3. Environmentalists believe that increased production of corn and soya

a. has destroyed rain forests.
b. may lead to the destruction of rain forests.
c. will lead to the destruction of rain forests.

4. Biofuels might

a. drive food prices up.
b. drive food prices down.
c. have little or no impact on food prices.

5. The increased production of palm oil

a. just affects the environment.

b.   just affects people.
c.   affects both people and the environment.

Say TURE or FALSE:

1.   Using bio fuels is one of solutions for decreasing the impact of global warming.
2.   The report produced by the investors expresses concern that many companies may not be fully aware of the potential pitfalls in the bio fuel sector.
3.   Production of corn and soya beans has decreased dramatically last year.
4.   Bio fuels can help balance climatic changes.
5.   Prices of foodstuffs may go up because of increase in bio fuel production.

Write the meanings of the words:

1.   Jeopardy 2) adverse 3) unrest 4) pitfall 5) efficiency

Exercise 4:

NEITHER A BORROWER NOR A LENDER BE

Both borrowers and lenders in the sub-prime mortgage market are wishing they had listened to the old saying: neither a borrower nor a lender be.

Last year people with poor credit ratings borrowed $605 billion in mortgages, a figure that is about 20% of the home-loan market. It includes people who cannot afford to meet the mortgage payments on expensive homes they have bought, and low-income buyers. In some cases, the latter could not even meet the first payment. Lenders include banks like HSBC, which may have lost almost $7 billion.

Both sides can be blamed. Lenders, after the 2-3 percentage point premium they could charge, offered loans, known as 'liar loans', with no down payments and without any income verification to people with bad credit histories. They believed that rising house prices would cover them in the event of default. Borrowers ignored the fact that interest rates would rise after an initial period.

One result is that default rates on these sub-prime mortgages reached 14% last year- a record. The problems in this market also threaten to spread to the rest of the mortgage market, which would reduce the flow of credit available to the shrinking numbers of consumers still interested in buying property.

So, the housing market will remain weak; borrowers with weak credit histories will find the credit window closed; people with adjustable-rate mortgages will have to spend less so they can meet their increased payments; tighter lending standards and falling home prices will reduce consumers' ability to tap the equity in their homes.

But as long as the labour market remains strong, which it has done despite job losses in housing-related industries, and as long as real incomes continue to go up, consumers might complain, but they are unlikely to go on a buyers' strike on a scale that will make this slowdown become a recession. Therefore, we should not be too worried, but, at the same time, we should be a bit cautious and watch closely how things develop.

Choose the best answer:

1. Sub-prime mortgage loans were offered

a. only to low income families.
b. to people who wanted to by very expensive houses.
c. to people with poor credit histories.

2. Who believed that rising house prices would cover them in the event of a default?

a. Borrowers
b. Lenders
c. Both

3. Borrowers have been caught out

a. because they lied when applying for the loan.
b. because house prices have risen.
c. because interest rates rise after a while.

4. According to the text, people with adjustable-rate mortgages

a. will not be able to get credit.
b. will have to economise.

c. have weak credit histories.

5. The housing market problems

a. could easily tip the counrty in recession.
b. are unlikely to tip the country into recession.
c. will cause a buyers' strike.

Say TRUE or FALSE:

1. People believe that rising house prices would cover them in the event of default.
2. One result is that default rates on these sub-prime mortgages reached 16% last year- a record.
3. The borrowers with weak credit histories will be able to get credit in future.
4. The writer is not worried about the housing market.
5. The old saying 'neither a borrower nor a lender be' is not remembered by many.

Write the meanings of the words:

1. Mortgage 2) expensive 3) equity 4) consumer 5) cautious

Exercise 5:

WITTGENSTEIN

In his thought-provoking work, Philosophical Investigations, Ludwig Wittgenstein uses an easily conceptualized scenario in an attempt to clarify some of the problems involved in thinking about the mind as something over and above the behaviors that it produces. Imagine, he says, that everyone has a small box in which they keep a beetle. No one is allowed to look in anyone else's box, only in their own. Over time, people talk about what is in their boxes and the word "beetle" comes to stand for what is in everyone's box.

Through this curious example, Wittgenstein attempts to point out that the beetle is very much like an individual's mind; no one can know exactly what it is like to be another person or experience things from another's perspective—look in someone else's "box"—but it is generally assumed that the mental workings of other people's minds are very similar to that of our own (everyone has a "beetle" which is more or less similar to everyone else's). However, it does not really matter—he argues—what is in the box or whether everyone indeed has a beetle, since there is no way of checking or comparing. In a sense, the word "beetle"—if it is to have any sense or meaning—simply means "what is in the box". From this point of view, the mind is simply "what is in the box", or rather "what is in your head".

Wittgenstein argues that although we cannot know what it is like to be someone else, to say that there must be a special mental entity called a mind that makes our experiences private, is wrong. His rationale is that he considers language to have meaning because of public usage. In other words, when we talk of having a mind—or a beetle—we are using a term that we have learned through conversation and public discourse (rooted in natural language). The word might be perceived differently in each of our minds, but we all agree that it signifies something; this allows us to develop language for talking about conceptualizations like color, mood, size and shape. Therefore, the word "mind" cannot be used to refer specifically to some entity outside of our individualized conception, since we cannot see into other people's boxes.

Choose the best answer:

1. Based on information in the passage, Wittgenstein apparently believes that

i. it is best to think of mental states as nothing over and above the behaviors they produce
ii. the public use of language is responsible for misconceptions about the mind
iii. through the use of precise language, it is possible to accurately describe the shared properties of the mind

a. i only
b. ii only
c. i and ii only
d. ii and iii only
e. i, ii, and iii

2. Which of the following literary devices best describes Wittgenstein's use of the "beetle in a box" scenario?

a. Authorial intrusion, characterized by a point at which the author speaks out directly to the reader.
b. Aphorism, characterized by the use of a concise statement that is made in a matter of fact tone to state a principle or an opinion that is generally understood to be a universal truth.
c. Amplification, characterized by the embellishment or extension of a statement in order to give it greater worth or meaning.
d. Allegory, characterized by the use of symbolic representation to convey the meaning of an often abstract concept.
e. Ambiguity, characterized by the expression of an idea in such a way that it becomes possible to glean more than one meaning from it.

3. Wittgenstein would most likely disagree with which of the following statements?

a. It is impossible to know another person's thoughts.
b. The mind is a special mental substance.
c. The color green may actually look different to everybody.
d. Words do not always accurately represent the things they symbolize.
e. It takes time for public discourse to create a new word with a common meaning.

4. As used in paragraph 3, which is the best synonym for discourse?

a. exchange
b. conversation
c. announcement
d. knowledge
e. setting

5. Based on his use of the "beetle in a box" comparison in the passage, it can be inferred that Wittgenstein might similarly compare a room full of people to a

a. deck of cards

b. box of chocolates
c. collection of rocks
d. library of books
e. group of drinking glasses filled with water

Say TRUE or FALSE:

1. The author compares people's mind with the beetle in box.
2. According to Wittgenstein, special mental entity called a mind that makes our experiences private.
3. The word "mind" cannot be used to refer specifically to some entity outside of our individualized conception, since we cannot see into other people's boxes.
4. Words do not always accurately represent the things they symbolize.
5. Working of people's mind is similar.

Write the meanings of the words:

1. Curious 2) perspective 3) discourse 4) entity 5) perceive

Given below are three passages. The first one is easy, the second one is of medium difficulty level, and the third one is quite difficult. Read and attempt answering the questions. Notice what makes them vary in their difficulty levels.

Passage 1

The Indian Premier League (IPL) is a professional Twenty20 cricket league in India contested during April and May of every year by 8 teams representing 8 cities of India. The league was founded by the Board of Control for Cricket in India (BCCI) in 2008, and is regarded as the brainchild of Lalit Modi, the founder and former commissioner of the league. IPL has an exclusive window in ICC Future Tours Programme.

The IPL is the most-attended cricket league in the world and in 2014 ranked sixth by average attendance among all sports leagues. In 2010, the IPL became the first sporting event in the world to be broadcast live on YouTube. The brand value of IPL in 2018 was US$6.3 billion, according to Duff & Phelps. According to BCCI, the 2015 IPL season contributed ?11.5 billion (US$182 million) to the GDP of the Indian economy.

There have been eleven seasons of the IPL tournament. The current IPL title holders are the Chennai Super Kings, who won the 2018 season.

Read the passage and choose the most appropriate option

Q1. Indian Premier League is considered whose brainchild?

a) Lalit Modi

b) Nirav Modi

c) Vineet Jain

d) Mukesh Ambani

Q2. How many seasons have been played of IPL till 2018?

a) 10

b) 12

c) 11

d) 9

Q3. What is the antonym of the world "professional" w.r.t it's usage in the passage?

a) Competent

b) Amateur

c) Master

d) Polished

Q4. In which year IPL became the first sporting event to be broadcast live on an online platform?

a) 2011

b) 2010

c) 2008

d) 2012

Q5. According to Duff & Phelps, the brand value of IPL in 2018 was

a) ?11.5 billion

b) US $182 million

c) ? 6.3 billion

d) US $6.3 billion

Passage 2

The 543 elected MPs will be elected from single-member constituencies using first-past-the-post voting. The President of India nominates an additional two members from the Anglo-Indian community if he believes the community is under-represented.

Eligible voters must be Indian citizens, 18 or older, an ordinary resident of the polling area of the constituency and possess a valid voter identification card issued by the Election Commission of India. Some people convicted of electoral or other offences are barred from voting.

Earlier there were speculations that the Modi Government might advance the 2019 general election to counter the anti-incumbency factor, however learning from its past blunder of preponing election made by the Vajpayee Government it decided to go into election as per the normal schedule which was announced by Election Commission of India (ECI) on 10 March 2019, after which Model Code of Conduct was applied with immediate effect.

Based on the passage, a few questions are given below. Choose the appropriate answers

Q1. Which word or phrase means "disapproval of current political officeholders" in the passage

a. First-past-the-post
b. Blunder
c. Anti-incumbency
d. Model Code of Conduct

Q2. Since when was the Model Code of Conduct applied with immediate effect?

a. 23rd May 2018
b. 10th March 2019
c. 10th March 2018
d. 11th March 2019

Q3. When does the President of India nominate an additional two members from the Anglo-Indian community?

a. When there are less than 543 elected MPs
b. When the Anglo-Indian community fails to send a representative
c. When the president believes that the Anglo-Indian community is over-represented
d. When the president believes that the Anglo-Indian community is under-represented

Q4. What are the mandatory requirements to vote in India?

   i. Must be an Indian citizen
  ii. Must be18 or older
 iii. Must have a valid criminal record
 iv. Must be an ordinary resident of the polling area of the constituency
  v. Must possess a valid voter identification card issued by the Election Commission of India

Choose the correct options
(i), (ii) (iii)
(ii) (i) (v) (iv)
(ii) (iii) (i) (iv) (v)
(ii) (iii) (iv) (v)

Q5. What is the apt meaning of "speculations" as per the passage?

a. Conjectures
b. Assumptions
c. Either (a) or (b)
d. Both (a) and (b)

Passage 3

Nature writing is nonfiction or fiction prose or poetry about the natural environment. Nature writing encompasses a wide variety of works, ranging from those that place primary emphasis on natural history facts (such as field guides) to those in which philosophical interpretation predominate. It includes natural history essays, poetry, essays of solitude or escape, as well as travel and adventure writing.

Nature writing often draws heavily on scientific information and facts about the natural world; at the same time, it is frequently written in the first person and incorporates personal observations of and philosophical reflections upon nature.

Modern nature writing traces its roots to the works of natural history that were popular in the second half of the 18th century and throughout the 19th. An important early figure was the "parson-naturalist" Gilbert White (1720 – 1793), a pioneering English naturalist and ornithologist. He is best known for his Natural History and Antiquities of Selborne (1789).

Q1. Nature writing emphasizes on
i. Historical facts about the nature
ii. Philosophical interpretations of the nature

iii. Scientific information and facts

Choose the most appropriate

a) None of the above

b) Only (i) and (ii)

c) All the above

d) Only (i) and (ii)

Q2. Based on the passage what is period to which the modern nature writing can be traced to

a) 1850 till 1999

b) 1850 to 1899

c) 1750 till 1899

d) 1750 till 1900

Q3. Which statement summarizes the above passage

a) The passage talks about the life and lessons of Gilbert White, a profound naturalist and ornithologist.

b) The passage talks about how the nature writing is missing in the modern era and needs to be revived.

c) The passage talks about from where the writers draw inspiration for nature writing, and how its importance is diminishing in the modern era.

d) The passage talks about what nature writing is, the different types of nature writing, its style, and about the roots and pioneer of modern nature writing.

Q4. Which word aptly describes the word "reflections" as used in the passage

a) Opinion

b) Reproduction

c) Images

d) None of the above

Q5. According to the passage, what kind of works are written as part of nature writing?

i. Natural history essays and essays of solitude or escape

ii. Poetry

iii. Travel and adventure writing

Choose the correct options

a) Only (i)

b) Only (i) and (ii)

c) Only (ii) and (iii)

d) All the above

WRITING

XII

WRITE!

Writing is an art. Not just creative writing but also technical writing demands a lot of time and effort. While creative writing has the liberty to be free of ties like grammar and punctuation, technical writing has no such liberty. One has to master the basics of the language to produce readable material.

What do professionals write?

- Reports
- Mails
- Memos
- Circulars
- Process techniques
- Research articles

The list is endless. Writing does not mean paper and a pen alone. Today e-writing is dominant. Whatever the case, the rules do not change. Some certain tips and tricks will make the task of writing easy.

DOs:

- Use small sentences. Break the ideas into smaller points and then draft the content.

- Keep the language and words simple. Using high-sounding words will mar the flow.
- Stick on to an order. A step-by-step explanation will make it easy for the readers to understand.
- Use connectives like ***hence; thus; therefore; as a result; but; nonetheless; however***
- Use clue phrases to structure your content.

  - The previous argument suggests that...
  - A good illustration of this point is...
  - Before evaluating this argument in detail, I will...
  - In response to this objection...
  - Firstly...Secondly...Thirdly...
  - To sum up what I have said so far...

- Split the content into smaller parts
- Use examples, illustrations, charts, graphs, or tables wherever necessary

DON'Ts:

- Avoid distracting examples or pictures
- Do not make lengthy sentences by adding connectives continuously
- Do not overthink or overwrite on one aspect alone. Try to keep a balance.
- Stick on to a word limit that will help you to write spot-on
- Acknowledge sources of references to avoid plagiarism

Make sure the content has a proper introduction and conclusion

PARAGRAPH WRITING

A Paragraph is a unit which consists of one or more sentences. It is a section of prose in which a particular topic is stated and developed. In other words it is a group of sentences, all of which focus on a single subject. A well-written paragraph possesses the characteristics described below:

1. It almost always contains a topic sentence that presents the subject of the paragraph.
2. The rest of the sentences of the paragraph relate to the topic sentence in one of the following ways-

    a. lead into/ up to it
    b. explain it, by either expanding or limiting its meaning
    c. support it
    d. support or explain one of the supporting sentences

3. The **topic sentence** mostly occurs at or near the beginning of the paragraph.
4. In the case of an introductory paragraph as part of bigger composition the topic sentence ordinarily occurs at or near the conclusion.
5. The topic sentence most often contains the main idea of the paragraph.
6. The three main components of a paragraph.

Unity

The most important thing to note while writing a paragraph is the fact that each paragraph is 'one whole'. In other words it has unity, which is the outcome of there being a single topic in each paragraph.

Cohesion

Cohesion refers to the way one sentence is grammatically related to another. It ensures a smooth transition.

Coherence

Coherence on the other hand, ensures 'thought unity' or 'sense unity' in a given piece of text. In other words it shows how various sentences in the text make sense together.

7. Paragraphs aimed for given effect should have varying lengths. The length is maintained according to the need and requirement of the reader, subject matter, writing style, variety and emphasis.

8. **The Importance of Newspapers**

Newspapers are the cheapest medium of information today. Also they are easily available to everybody. Newspapers are an important means of educating people. Those who read newspapers become well-informed about current affairs. The Editorial page discusses important questions and problems of national and international importance. Letters to the Editor give us the views of the readers on various subjects. The Sports Page gives interesting information about games and sports. Newspapers also contain advertisements. These advertisements are very useful for businessmen and those who are in search of jobs. The matrimonial column helps people in finding the right kind of husband or wife. Thus newspapers are useful for almost everyone.

EXERCISES

Write paragraphs on the following:

1. Impact of mobile phones on youth.
2. Measures to avoid plastics.
3. Hockey – the national game threatened by cricket.
4. Professional ethics
5. Career options for Management Students

WRITING ANALYTICAL ESSAYS

Analytical paragraphs respond to logical issues. It provides supportive evidences and answers the question '*How?*' Writing analytical paragraphs involves 7 basic components.

- **Topic Sentence** – It is usually the first sentence of the content. It connects directly to the theme of the content and provides scope for arguments.
- **Introduction of Evidence** – The evidence can be presented in a sentence or two, emphasizing the aspects to be focused on.
- **Analysis or Discussion** – This includes the main content that points out the various issues to be discussed, possible solutions to the issues and few supporting points for those reasonable solutions.
- **Conclusion** – This should tie back to the topic sentence and should summarize the overall content.

Examples:

1. TERRORISM

Terrorism is a worldwide phenomenon. It could be defined as the low-intensity warfare against the common man and the State. Terrorism in India has made us believe to coexist with virtuous path during the past decade.

What actually is terrorism-it is the spread of terror, as the name indicates. It could be spread, just by frightening the other, either by loot or killing. Terrorism at home has surpassed the latter variety, someone killing indiscriminately for pride or power. It has taken recourse to slow but sure poisoning of India by a continuous war of nerves, with our neighbour Pakistan exporting the act by training of unemployed infidels.

The objective of terrorism is to make people run out of the territory. Once terror spreads, people run away for cover thereby the perpetrator of the crime achieves the objective. This menace needs to be shelved out in Kashmir with an obvious intent of annexing Kashmir. For, if the caste Hindus flee and the ballot caste, there is no chance for a vote for India.

Terrorists have struck the bait across the state during 1990s, so much so that eighty per cent of Hindu community has fled from the scene to make home elsewhere. Such tragedy made people homeless in their own country. Now, new band of terrorists have spread hatred wings in other parts of the world. It appears the entire world has to work with constant vigil, tooth and nail, against the menace, before the orgy of destruction spree through the length and breathe of the world.

Methinks terrorism could be wiped off the scene provided the think-tank of the developed and developing world unites for the cause. No country could face the scenario and end this plan of destruction.

1. **TECHNOLOGY – BOON OR BANE?**

The overt observation of some knowledgeable persons who passionately feel concerned for the welfare of humanity, in the wake of scientific strides and technological triumphs, laments that "technology creates more problems than it solves". Their concern echoes the similar sentiments of thinkers like J.G.Ballard for whom, "technology dictates the languages in which we speak and think. Either we use those languages or we remain mute", and for Omar Bradley "our technology has already outstripped our ability to control it". Despite these jarring notes, technology has acquired a halo that is almost impossible to shake off.

Who can deny the robust role and range of technology that we experience in our every day life. If we care to look at the scintillating side of technology, we find space technology and its applications provide useful data for natural disaster monitoring, solving environment problems, improve telecommunications and provide other basic services. Through fax, e-Mail and the Internet, information technology has outstripped all barriers that time and space had placed in man's search for instant information. Though electronic information is hard to control, yet the individual newsgatherer is visible and vulnerable. The latest in the success story is the likely boom that bio-technology promises to unfold in the years to come. Rightly, biotechnology is being seen by scientists and entrepreneurs alike as the next big thing with the potential to revolutionise the fields of agriculture, health and medicine. The promises are many: disease-resistant and high-yield crops that could solve the world's food problems; new medicines and drug delivery systems to cure diseases and prevent genetically inherited disorders; and new enzymes that make industrial production more efficient and cost-effective.

For ages the axiom, nothing is good or bad but thinking makes it so, was the golden rule that moulded human perceptions and concrete actions. With the advent of science and technology, and their subsequent sway over human ideas, intuitions and ideologies, it is now 'the use or abuse' of technology that renders it either a blessing or a bane for humanity that lives and survives on the ever- spreading tentacles of technology. In short, it is the technology that rules the roost now and keeps its ambience alive all the time in various manifestations. With the frontiers of technology influencing all aspects of life, both in terms of time and space, it is anybody's guess as to what the future holds in store for humanity, that has become so enamoured of technology.

If the past is any guide, one can learn a lot from the happenings of the 20th century, that used and abused scientific and technological achievements for increasing physical comforts and living standards, as also for fighting the two world wars, resorting to nuclear bombing and land mines and other means of mass deaths and destruction, dislocation of millions resulting in untold misery and suffering. In the face of so much good that we expect from science and technology, scientist warn that if we do not change our ways, our civilisation is not likely to survive.

Man's greed, aided and abetted by science and technology, has already over-exploited and abused the earth's material resources and destroyed its ecosystems. Forests are vanishing and there is increased desertification, the seas and oceans are stained with death because of the poisons that we have poured into them. We have even polluted the rain with poisonous smoke from our industrial chimneys. We have not only raped the soil and denigrated the ecosystems, but also lost touch with our inner self.

There is no denying that our cares and concerns are being controlled by technology, in its various forms and facets. Whether in company or in solitude, technology has come to occupy a pivotal place in our day to day life. If the despots use it to perpetuate their repressive rule, the terrorists have employed it to explode symbols of progress. With no end to man's rapacious nature in sight, technology has become a hand-maiden of unscrupulous exploiters of natural resources and immoral traders of wild life species.

Technology as it reigns supreme over our intellect and imagination, is redefining human relations. In a bid to hit the jackpot, or make a quick buck, the individual has lost his identity and, in the bargain, has fallen an easy prey to alienation and estrangement. Smarting under physical fatigue and mental stress, he has become a victim of the phenomenon of being an "outsider" among his own people. Despite a host of benefits that technology has conferred on us in varying degrees, the onslaught of anger and angst is very much conspicuous. If today we are scared of some impending disaster, it is because technology has given such powers to individuals and groups which even the demons or deities of mythology did not enjoy.

We are standing at the threshold where technology as a source of boon or brazenness is staring in our face. In moments of introspection, we must bear in mind what Aldous Huxley had said: "technological progress has merely provided us with more efficient means for going backwards".

3. FRIENDS

A friend in need is a friend indeed is a proverb that stands true always. In our day to day work, we come across so many persons and all of them are not our friends.

God does not create friends. We acquire them. How are friends made? Friends have some qualities in common. They are generally of the same age group. Their aptitudes and interest, likes and dislikes are generally common. They may live nearby, may go to the same school or may be doing the same work. Good friends know all about one another. There would be no secrets among them. They love one another better than their relative.

There are different kinds of friends. True and faithful friends, casual friends and false or fair-weather friends. A true and faithful friend has certain qualities, which you should also have. It is correctly said that to have a friend you should be one.

True friends are like one soul, living in two bodies. They are attached so much to one another. A real friend is one who comes to you, when all others have left. Never a true one flatters you. He may at times frown upon you. A friend's frown is said to be better than a foe's praise. An old friend is like old wine. He is a stimulating force. An old friend is one, on whom one can always rely. He stands by you, at all times and shares you joys and sorrows. It is an unbroken friendship till the last.

In our day to day affairs, we come across so many, who become friends for a purpose. There are also other type of friends, who are casual friends, whom we meet on our travels in buses and the trains. They are friends with whom we exchange so many views. But at the end of the journey, each goes his own way and the casual friendship is also gone.

There are fair-weather friends. They are sycophants. They praise you to skies and linger around you as long as you enjoy property and power. When fortune turns against you, they would be nowhere to be seen.

Friendship spreads on. Even in you have a thousand friends you can still add one more. It is said that house can be known by the friends who frequent it. Know his friends and you know the man. Mahatma Gandhi says adversity is the crucible test for friendship. You know your real friend, only when he stands by you, in times of adversity. It is said prosperity makes friends. Adversity tries them.

Examples of true friends are many in our Puranas and history. Karna, the first son of Kunthi was a true friend of Duryodhana, for whose sake he sacrificed his life. The story of Sudhama and Lord Krishna is another example of real friendship.

Friendship is said to be an art and very few persons are said to be born with a natural gift for it. It is said that friendship multiplies our joys and divides our grief's. Your life is blessed, if you have a faithful friend. Ion this world of wilderness every one of us requires a true friend. But beware; a friend of all is a friend of none.

4. **CORRUPTION**

Now-a-days corruption can be seen everywhere. It is like cancer in public life, which has not become so rampant and perpetuated overnight, but in course of time. A country where leaders like Mahatma Gandhi, Sardar Patel, Lai Bahadur Shastri and Kamraj have taken birth and led a value-based is now facing the problem of corruption.

When we talk of corruption in public life, it covers corruption in politics, state governments, central governments, "business, industry and so on. Public dealing counters in most all government offices are the places where corruption most evident. If anybody does not pay for the work it is sure work won't be done.

People have grown insatiable appetite for money in them and they can go to any extent to get money. Undoubtedly they talk of morality and the importance of value-based life but that is for outer show. Their inner voice is something else.

It is always crying for money. It has been seen the officers who are deputed to look into the matters of corruption turn out to be corrupt. Our leaders too are not less corrupt. Thus the network of corruption goes on as usual and remains undeterred.

Corruption is seen even in the recruitment department where appointments are ensured through reliable middle agencies. Nexus between politicians and bureaucrats works in a very sophisticated manner. Nexus does also exist between criminals and police.

Everybody knows that criminals have no morals, hence nothing good can we expect from them. But police are supposed to be the symbol of law and order and discipline. Even they are indulged in corruption. This is more so because they enjoy unlimited powers and there is no action against them even on complaints and sufficient proof of abuse of office atrocities and high handedness.

Corruption can be need-based or greed-based. Better governance can at least help to check need-based corruption. Better governance can check greed based corruption also because punishment for the corrupt will be very effective and prompt in a better-governed country.

The steps should be taken to correct the situation overall. Declarations of property and assets of the government employees are made compulsory and routine and surprise inspections and raids be conducted at certain intervals.

Though it seems very difficult to control corruption but it is not impossible. It is not only the responsibility of the government but ours too. We can eliminate corruption if there will be joint effort. We must have some high principles to follow so that we may be models for the coming generation. Let us take a view to create an atmosphere free from corruption. That will be our highest achievement as human beings.

5. **CHILD LABOUR**

Child labor refers to the employment of children. This practice is illegal in many countries. In rich countries it is considered as a human rights violation.

Child labor goes back a long way in time. During the Victorian era, many young children were made to work in factories and mines and as chimney sweeps. Child labor played an important role in the Industrial Revolution. Charles Dickens worked at the age of 12 in the Blacking Factory, while his family was in debtor's prison. In those days, children as young as four were employed in production factories with dangerous working conditions.

With universal schooling and the introduction of concepts like human rights and child rights, slowly child labor fell into disrepute. The first general laws against child labor, the Factory Acts, were passed in Britain in the first half of the 19th century. Children younger than nine were not allowed to work.

Poverty is the main reason why child labor exists. Children bring in additional income which is much needed and so parents send them to work.

Child labor is common in poorer parts of the world. Children may work in factories, sweatshops, mines, fields, hotels, match factories, or in households. Some children work as guides for tourists and may end up getting sexually abused by them as happens in places like Goa and Kerala.

As many children work in the informal sector they manage to escape the scrutiny of the labor inspectors and the media. According to UNICEF, there are an estimated 158 million children aged 5 to 14 engaged in child labor worldwide. In 1999, the Global March against Child Labor, the movement, began. Thousands of people marched together to spread the message against child labor.

The march, which started on January 17, 1998, built immense awareness and culminated at the ILO Conference in Geneva. It resulted in the draft of the ILO Convention against the worst forms of child labor. The following year, the Convention was unanimously adopted at the ILO Conference in Geneva.

Child labor is still widely prevalent in India. It is estimated that there are between 70 and 80 million child laborers in India. Though there are laws banning child labor they are blatantly ignored even by educated and well-informed people. Young children not yet in their teens often work for 20 hours a day in sweatshops and are paid only a pittance.

In many developed countries, there is a move to boycott goods and products made by employing child labor. Child labor is a cruel practice. Childhood is a time to play and be carefree, enjoying the company of other children. A child is not equipped to work like an adult so this evil practice should be banned and the government should see that no child is deprived of an education because of poverty.

Activities:

1. Write a short essay analyzing the advantages and disadvantages of mobile phones.

2. Draft a brief essay analyzing the effects of global warming.

3. Write an essay on how sexual abuses could be prevented.

4. Analyse the various consequences of dieting.

5. How can one improve ones communication skills? Analyse.

XIII
HOW TO DRAFT A PROFESSIONAL EMAIL

Emails are the most commonly used tool to communicate in professional environments. It is faster, easier to access, and handy to use. While emails have many advantages, the biggest disadvantage is that once a mail is sent, it cannot be recalled. A mail with mistakes, when sent, fails to make a good impression on the sender. Here are a few tips to make emails effective.

- Use a meaningful subject line. DO NOT send a mail without a subject.
- Address the receiver appropriately. The most commonly used addressal phrase is **Dear Sir/Ma'am**. However, you may use the receiver's name if the person is familiar to you. A professional environment expects addressal like **Hello Mr Jones.** If the person is a regular communicator and is already on a first-name basis, continue using the person's first name.
- Keep the content short and to the point. If needed, attach documents to explain further.
- Check if the necessary files are attached if you have mentioned attachments.
- Use polite words. Do not use slang.
- Re-read before sending the mail out.
- Always use an appropriate signature to sign out. The most appropriate signature will carry your full name, designation, and company name.

SAMPLE EMAIL 1:

Below is a sample of how to write an email confirming your first day of work.

Hello Ms Smith,

Thank you for the offer letter. I am looking forward to getting started in a couple of weeks. I am writing to confirm that my first day of work will be on Thursday, Nov. 12. I have already read through the documents you sent me the other day. Please let me know if there is anything else I can do to prepare for my first day of work.

I look forward to meeting the whole team soon. Thanks again for giving me this exciting opportunity.

Thanks & regards,

Lisa Connor.

SAMPLE EMAIL 2:

Reporting to a manager or the boss regarding work updates is a normal process in every organization. Some managers want daily reports from their subordinates regarding the work process. The main aim behind this is it brings a habit of accountability in employees, and at the same time, the progress of the work will also be measured regularly.

Tips to write an email to the manager regarding work updates

- Describe all the recent updates which have taken place in that particular work. Mention previous updates only when they are required.
- Keep the email simple and short.
- Involve other members who participated in fulfilling the work. You can involve them by adding in CC.
- Attach the required documents.
- Always ask for feedback from your manager.

__Sub__: Update on XYZ process reg.

Dear Mr. Venkat,

Here I would like to inform you regarding the recent progress in our work. With the support of all the team members, the process will soon be completed. At this juncture, we need your valuable feedback on the work we have done so far.

Please find the attached documents related to the work progress.

Thanks & regards,

Bala

Team Lead - XYZ Process

SAMPLE 3:

Applying for leave is a common scenario. However, it is one mail where people fail to draft properly. Below is a sample mail.

Subject: Request for time off from 15-December to 18-December

Dear Mr. Venkat,

I would like to request time off from 15-December to 18-December next week. I have to travel to my hometown for the holidays and would like to leave before the last-minute rush. We have already discussed this in our meeting today, and my absence will not impact the continuity of our delivery to the client. Nonetheless, I will be available over the phone and by email during this time.

I request you to approve my leave request. I shall convey the same to the HR department.

Thanks,

Bala,

Digital marketer

XIV
WRITING REPORTS

WHAT IS A BUSINESS REPORT?

A business report is an official document drafted to present facts, statistical data, and research findings. It can either be to explain new projects or to explain the progress and outcomes of a completed project.

The following steps will guide you through creating a powerful business report.

- Define what you aim to achieve with the report and how you plan to present it.
- Your company may have a specific format for writing reports. Ask your supervisor or check the company's handbook to find it.
- You should include a table of contents page only if the report is long and contains sub-sections.
- You should write the abstract so that even if a person does not read the entire report, this page can give them a clear and detailed idea of the entire thing.
- Give an introduction to specify the purpose of writing the report along with a brief idea of the main argument. You can also include some background on the topic.
- State your methodology, the sources of information, type of data (qualitative or quantitative), channels of receiving information, etc.
- Include stats, facts, and graphs to portray the information. Align the data into various headings and subheadings. Use pointers, bulleted, or numbered whenever required.

- End your report with a compelling conclusion. This should be drawn from previously stated findings, recommendations, or suggestions.

If you have added any data or statistics in your report, you must give due credit to the original author. Else, it counts as plagiarism, which is a punishable offence.

CHARACTERISTICS OF A GOOD BUSINESS REPORT

Given below is a sample report.
1. Report on the Fire Accident
By
Sam
The Safety Engineer

Hyudai Motor Company LTD.
Chennai
Hyudai Motor Company LTD.
58, NEHRU STREET, CHENNAI – 108
To: The Managing Director
From: The Safety Engineer
05 June 2022
Sir,
Sub: A report on the fire accident in our Factory – reg.,
With reference to your intimation dated 03 Jan 2022; a detailed study has been made on the fire accident that took place on the 2nd of this month in our factory.

On the above mentioned date, a huge fire had broken out around 11 a.m. in our Welding Department. It spread so quickly that it consumed fairly a large number of tools and spare parts. Above all, Mr.Murugan, our chief welder was also badly hurt. Luckily he was the only person working at that time as the other workers had gone for tea break. Immediately, fire men were summoned and they extinguished the fire after battling for about half-an-hour. Mr.Murugan was hospitalized and he is now recovering fast.

Under investigation, it is found that the fire broke out because of a short circuit in the main line. As Mr. Murugan had been welding at that time, the fire had spread quickly. In addition, the wires had worn out and needed replacement. All these had resulted in the devastating fire. The total loss is estimated to be nearly Rs.1, 50,000.

To avoid such mishaps in the future, it is recommended that

- Wiring should be replaced and be checked at regular intervals
- Enough fire extinguishers must be kept handy.
- Automatic fire extinguishing sprays can be installed.
- Proper fuses should be used to avoid excess flow.
- Employees should be given proper training with regard to the use of electrical components and fire extinguishers.

If all these measures are taken, definitely such accidents can be prevented in future and thereby, great loss to human as well other resources could be averted.
Yours Faithfully
Sam

Safety Engineer

2. REPORT ON INDUSTRIAL VISIT

REPORT ON INDUSTRIAL VISIT

On

01-Mar-2022

Prepared By

Sekar

The Class Representative

XYZ College of Management

Chennai

Submitted to

The Head of the Department

Department of Management Studies

XYZ College of Management

Chennai

05-Mar-22

Sekar

The Class Representative

XYZ of Management

Chennai

The Head of the Department

Department of Management Studies

XYZ College of Management

Chennai

Dear Sir,

Sub: Report on the One – Day industrial visit

On receiving the letter of permission from Hyundai Motors Limited, Chennai 108, 61 students with two faculty members went on an industrial visit to the factory on 01-03-22. We all assembled at the college at 8 a.m. and left the college in a van. We reached the factory at 10 o'clock. The HR received us at the entrance and gave a brief introduction to the factory. Then he took us around from one section to the next and explained the process involved in the making of motors. The workers were doing the work concentrated. He showed various duties performed by employees in different departments. The visit came to an end at 3.00 p.m.

We left the premises at 3.30 p.m. It was an informative, interesting and successful visit. We express our thanks to the Principal who permitted us to go on the visit, the faculty members who accompanied the officials and us who explained the various departments. Behalf the students I request you to arrange more industrial visit for students which can practically train the students.

Thanking You
    Yours faithfully
    (Signature)
    Sekar
    The Class Representative

Exercises:

1) Your class has recently visited Blue Elephant Advertising , Chennai. Submit a report to the Head of the Department detailing the visit.

2) Write a report to the chairman of Get Well Hospital about the fire accident that happened in the hospital assuming yourself as the HR Manager.

3) You are the Marketing Manager of an automobile company, which is planning to introduce cars in an affordable prize, especially for college students. Submit a report to the CEO about the feasibitilies.

XV
ENGLISH FOR MARKETING & ADVERTISEMENT

Marketing and advertisement are powerful tools to take products and services to the public. If the tools are used properly, the business is sure to succeed. What makes marketing and advertisement effective? The answer is simple - good language. The English language is known for its great deal of vocabulary. Without a rich vocabulary, advertisement becomes lame. It cannot make a way for a brand into consumer markets.

The topic of advertising is always very controversial. People have a lot of hazy ideas on what gets someone to respond to an advertisement. Some advertisements have eye catching graphics and some are entertaining and humorous to attract the people to get responses. But, direct response marketers know what works and what doesn't work because they test everything. They care only about responses and they know what gets the best response. Here are some very useful insights from the direct response marketers.

Rule 1: Know your advertising objective

Once the objective is known, everything in your advertisement should be designed to accomplish that objective.

Rule 2: Get Their Attention

Crafting a headline that is relevant to the product or service will grab the attention of the people and increase their responses. Good headlines generally fall into three basic categories. The first type of headline is called a self-interest headline.

This type of headline spells out a benefit that the buyer will receive. An example of this type of headline would be -- "TAKE CARE"- Grainier products This clearly shows the reader that there is a benefit of taking care of appearance.

The second category is referred to as a news headline because it promises the reader something newsworthy. "Google Adds New Features to the Google Toolbar for Firefox ". The news in this headline is that there are new features that are much improved over the last ones.

The third category is a curiosity headline. These headlines are designed to make a reader want to continue to the body copy in order to learn more. An example of this would be

"5 Things Your Health Insurance company Doesn't Want You To Know"

Rule 3: Use Plain English

Eliminating big words with lots of syllables and technical jargon and using simple words

will allow the people to understand about the product clearly.

Rule4: Write About the Benefits

Features describe and benefits sell. Writing only about the features of the product will not be advisable. Along with the features , benefits of each features should be provided for the customer. These four rules are very useful to create any type of advertisements.

Below are few taglines of popular brands.

- Disneyland: "The happiest place on Earth."
- Nike: "Just do it."
- De Beers: "A diamond is forever."
- MasterCard: "There are some things money can't buy. For everything else, there's MasterCard."
- BMW: "The ultimate driving machine."
- Uber: "Move the way you want."
- Kentucky Fried Chicken: "Finger lickin' good."
- Toyota: "Let's go places."
- Raymond: "The complete man."
- Amul: "Taste of India"

These taglines are catchy, short, and explains the brand. Try framing a few taglines for products of your choice.

Happy writing!

XVI
Fun Activities

1. Here is a fun activity. Given below is a Word Search puzzle with several words related to marketing and advertisement. Spot as many as you can.

Marketing

```
Z  I  M  Y  P  U  R  W  I  R  G  R  K  L  F  Z  P  V  R  W  T  Z  N  C
Q  B  X  L  A  T  V  J  Y  B  A  P  F  A  X  Y  F  K  H  L  S  Q  L  U
U  T  N  F  N  J  U  K  B  F  E  C  A  I  U  C  V  D  X  D  E  U  L  S
I  N  D  O  P  O  O  B  V  E  Y  U  M  W  Q  P  W  L  M  K  I  Q  O  T
E  O  E  C  I  V  I  V  R  V  Z  G  W  D  S  X  Q  U  F  K  T  R  V  O
N  I  Z  Q  H  T  W  T  P  W  N  F  K  C  J  E  T  T  Z  G  I  O  U  M
G  T  J  D  S  N  A  I  A  I  F  M  P  D  G  X  Y  C  I  N  N  L  V  E
R  C  K  R  N  T  T  T  C  E  N  L  A  J  O  L  U  Q  I  U  E  A  R
E  A  R  N  O  Q  H  E  N  H  I  L  S  U  H  N  Q  D  X  T  T  V  T  Z
O  F  O  U  I  Q  K  J  H  E  X  N  Q  C  E  E  G  O  L  E  R  F  E  Y
H  S  W  X  T  R  N  Z  K  H  I  N  U  M  T  Y  K  R  M  K  O  O  K  G
I  I  M  K  A  J  E  C  S  M  O  R  P  M  H  L  X  P  D  R  P  H  R  R
M  T  A  M  L  J  S  L  D  I  T  O  O  X  M  V  B  N  U  A  P  W  A  A
O  A  E  I  E  Z  A  P  T  R  W  B  E  S  D  O  V  V  H  M  O  P  M  V
W  S  T  Q  R  O  D  C  T  E  C  L  H  O  E  Q  C  Q  C  K  I  M  D  W
S  E  U  T  G  M  U  A  R  C  R  C  Q  W  Z  L  V  B  R  E  O  I  I  D
O  X  S  E  E  D  B  M  R  C  X  W  T  Y  T  Q  A  Q  X  T  M  B  T  E
C  C  T  J  O  B  E  N  T  O  N  D  E  M  A  N  D  S  K  Q  S  W  I  L
I  H  N  R  X  N  L  Q  A  D  V  E  R  T  I  S  I  N  G  C  E  R  N  B
E  A  P  F  T  B  K  S  X  U  B  S  C  J  B  H  E  Y  V  I  X  O  V  D
T  N  X  C  A  V  W  P  G  O  A  Z  L  Y  H  E  D  Q  I  U  R  Q  N  Y
Y  G  H  K  G  L  K  A  R  Q  N  K  T  C  L  Z  A  Y  T  F  C  U  R  X
N  E  S  S  E  N  I  S  U  B  Q  L  N  V  N  J  N  J  R  D  U  T  V  J
J  R  H  X  Y  I  K  B  B  W  I  S  K  B  I  Q  T  S  I  Q  S  P  K  E
```

COMMUNICATION	ADVERTISING	BUSINESS
CUSTOMER	EMPOWERMENT	EXCHANGE
GOALS	MARKET	MARKETING
MARKETING MIX	ONDEMAND	OPPORTUNITIES
PRODUCT	PRODUCTION	RELATIONSHIP
SALESORIENTATION	SATISFACTION	SOCIETY
TEAMWORK		

Activity -2

Create an advertisement of your own with proper slogan for the following products.

1. Nike shoes

2. Branded Perfumes

3. IPod

4. Digital Camera

5. Cadbury coco bar

6. Coco cola

7. Amul butter

8.Apple iphone.

9.Arun Ice cream

10. Mercedes Benz car

Activity - 3

Create your own catchy headings for the following advertisements

1

2

3

References

This book has been compiled with references from several print and web sources. A few are listed below.

1. Sweeney, Simon. *Communicating in Business: A Short Course for Business English Students: Cultural Diversity and Socializing, Using the Telephone, Presentations, Meetings and Negotiations.* Cambridge University Press, 2004.
2. Geffner, Andrea B. *Business English.* Barron's, 2004.
3. "Sample Test Questions." Sample Test Questions, https://www.ielts.org/for-test-takers/sample-test-questions.
4. Kobiruzzaman, M M. "Business Report Example for Students- Business Report Sample for Students." Newsmoor, 3 Apr. 2022, https://newsmoor.com/business-report-example-and-sample-for-students-pdf/.
5. "Marketing Word Search." WordMint, https://wordmint.com/public_puzzles/30850.
6. S, Surbhi. "What Is Business Report? Example and Format." Business Jargons, 12 May 2022, https://businessjargons.com/business-report.html.